SEARCH & RESCUE

BY S.L. HAMILTON

A&D Xtreme
An Imprint of Abdo Publishing | www.abdopublishing.com

Visit us at
www.abdopublishing.com

Published by Abdo Publishing Company, a division of ABDO, PO Box 398166, Minneapolis, Minnesota 55439. Copyright ©2016 by Abdo Consulting Group, Inc. International copyrights reserved in all countries. No part of this book may be reproduced in any form without written permission from the publisher. A&D Xtreme™ is a trademark and logo of Abdo Publishing Company.

Printed in the United States of America, North Mankato, Minnesota.
052015
092015

 PRINTED ON RECYCLED PAPER

Editor: John Hamilton
Graphic Design: Sue Hamilton
Cover Design: Sue Hamilton
Cover Photo: Corbis
Interior Photos: AP-pgs 8, 9, 16-17, 18-19, & 20-21; Corbis-pgs 4-5, 14-15, 22, 23, & 26-27; FEMA/Andrea Booher-pg 24, FEMA/Jocelyn Augustino-pg 25 (top), FEMA/Bri Rodriguez-pg 25 (bottom); Granger-pg 6; National Naval Aviation Museum-pg 7 (top); Poudre Fire Authority of Fort Collins, CO-pg 1; U.S. Air Force-pgs 7 (middle & bottom) & 12-13; U.S. Coast Guard-pgs 2-3, 10-11 & 30-31; U.S. Navy-pgs 28-29 & 32.

Websites
To learn more about Xtreme Jobs, visit booklinks.abdopublishing.com. These links are routinely monitored and updated to provide the most current information available.

Library of Congress Control Number: 2015930952

Cataloging-in-Publication Data

Hamilton, S.L.
  Search & rescue / S.L Hamilton.
    p. cm. -- (Xtreme jobs)
  ISBN 978-1-62403-759-7
  1. Search and rescue operations--Juvenile literature. 2. Rescue work--Juvenile literature.
  I. Title.
  363.34--dc23
                                                2015930952

CONTENTS

SEARCH & RESCUE

Search and rescue (SAR) teams find and return to safety people who have survived an emergency situation. Search and rescue personnel often risk their own lives to help others. Some are volunteers. Others are professionals. They know how incredible it is to save someone who may have died without their help.

XTREME FACT – 98% of lost people are found alive and uninjured.

HISTORY

Search and rescue work began with family and friends helping each other. Wilderness searches and natural disasters have long brought people together to help when men, women, and children are lost or hurt.

Bombed ships and downed aircraft drew attention to the importance of search and rescue teams during wartime. Governments invested large amounts of money into training rescuers and improving technology. These people and their equipment are vital to saving important human and military resources.

A PBY Catalina flying boat rescue.

XTREME FACT - *Flying military air-sea rescues were called "Dumbo missions." They were named after the Disney elephant who could fly. Modified B-29 bombers dropped A-3 lifeboats. An A-3 could carry 15 people. It had food, water, and a small engine.*

A-3 Lifeboat

An SB-29 bomber drops a self-righting A-3 lifeboat.

TRAINING

Search and rescue courses are available in most towns and cities. Training may involve searches on land, water, air, or all three areas.

SAR team members train for a mine rescue.

XTREME FACT – The National Association for Search and Rescue (NASAR) and Community Emergency Response Team (CERT) programs train SAR members.

Education and equipment are different for rescues conducted in cities. New tools such as drones are used to view collapsed buildings.

A member of International Search and Rescue (ISAR) tests an unmanned aerial vehicle (UAV) for use in urban disasters.

Wilderness rescues often include survival training. SAR team members may be outside in extreme conditions for a long time.

SAR team members train for ice water rescues.

9

Air-Sea SAR

Air-sea search and rescue involves finding and helping people who have survived an emergency water landing in a plane. It also means helping people on sinking or disabled ships. Air-sea rescuers may search in helicopters, floatplanes, boats, or even submarines.

XTREME FACT – One of the United States Coast Guard's main missions is air-sea search and rescue. The Coast Guard uses some of the world's best technology to locate victims. They also learn to search or "scan" the old-fashioned way, using binoculars or simply their own eyes.

GROUND SAR

Ground search and rescue teams provide inland rescues. These often involve lost or injured children, hikers, campers, boaters, or people with mental health issues. Local areas set up their own training based on the challenges faced by the professional and volunteer team members.

United States Air Force pararescuemen, together with Arizona search and rescue crews, perform a high-angle rescue at the Grand Canyon.

XTREME FACT – The "Hug-a-Tree and Survive" program is taught to young people by SAR team members. The basic rule is to stay put until a searcher finds you.

MOUNTAIN SAR

Mountain search and rescue teams face fierce challenges. Temperatures may drop far below freezing. There may be high winds and blinding snow. Victims may have fallen to nearly unreachable places. They may be very cold, unconscious, or have broken bones or other serious injuries. Helicopters may be called in to help. However, helicopters cannot fly at very high altitudes, in high winds, fog, or heavy snow. Mountain search and rescue often requires team members on the ground. SAR teams regularly use dogs to help them locate lost people.

XTREME FACT – Helicopter rotors need air to provide lift. At high mountain altitudes, the air is too thin for the rotors to keep the vehicle in the air. A turbine-engined rescue helicopter can reach 25,000 feet (7,620 m), but its hover limit is only about 13,800 feet (4,206 m).

CAVE SAR

Trying to move an injured person in a cave is very difficult. Many cave search and rescue personnel are spelunkers themselves. Different types of caves require different kinds of gear. Rescuers need to know a cave's geology. They also must have knowledge of engineering, ropework, and trauma medicine.

MINE & TUNNEL SAR

Mine and tunnel search and rescue situations require a knowledge of many underground hazards. Toxic gas, smoke, fire, explosions, cave-ins, and flooding are all problems these SAR teams must know how to handle.

Members of a search and rescue team train for helping an injured worker in a mine in Germany.

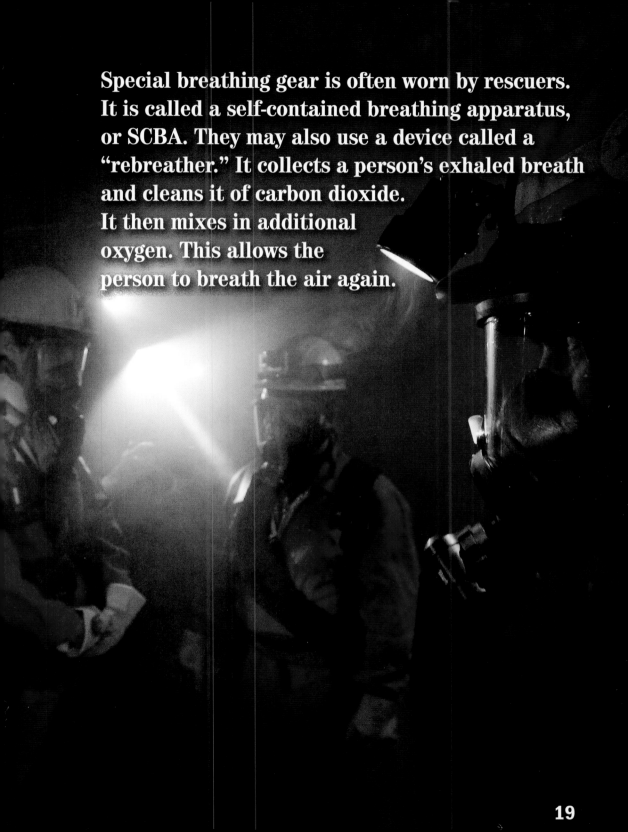

Special breathing gear is often worn by rescuers. It is called a self-contained breathing apparatus, or SCBA. They may also use a device called a "rebreather." It collects a person's exhaled breath and cleans it of carbon dioxide. It then mixes in additional oxygen. This allows the person to breath the air again.

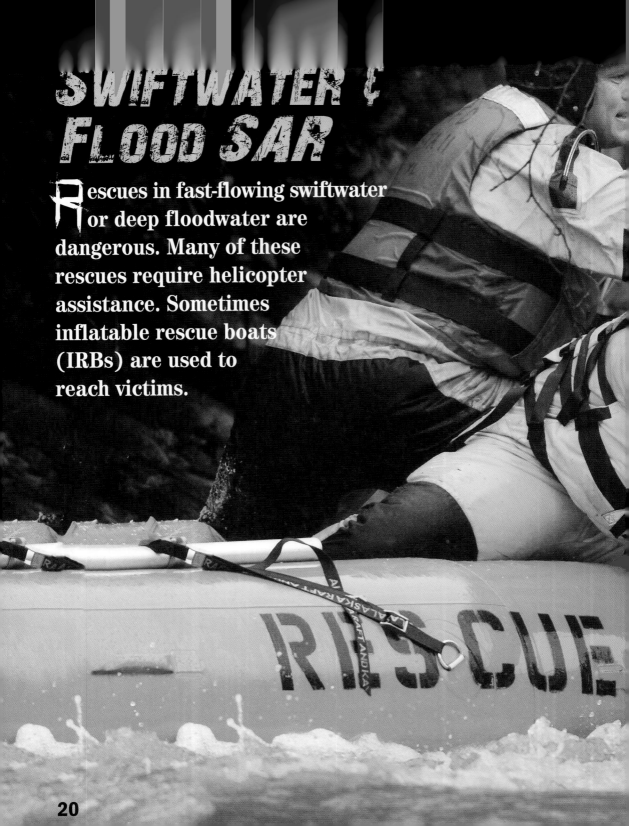

SWIFTWATER & FLOOD SAR

Rescues in fast-flowing swiftwater or deep floodwater are dangerous. Many of these rescues require helicopter assistance. Sometimes inflatable rescue boats (IRBs) are used to reach victims.

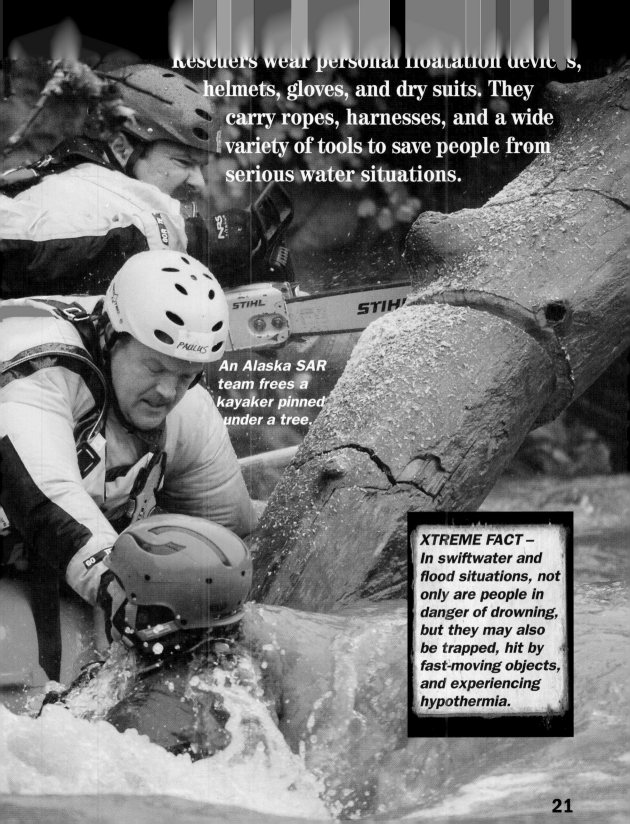

Rescuers wear personal floatation devices, helmets, gloves, and dry suits. They carry ropes, harnesses, and a wide variety of tools to save people from serious water situations.

An Alaska SAR team frees a kayaker pinned under a tree.

XTREME FACT – In swiftwater and flood situations, not only are people in danger of drowning, but they may also be trapped, hit by fast-moving objects, and experiencing hypothermia.

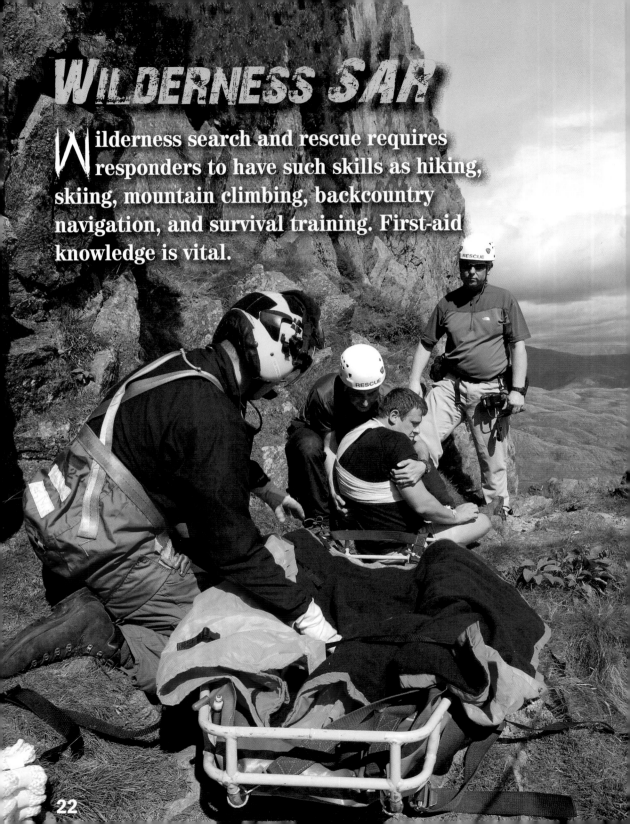

WILDERNESS SAR

Wilderness search and rescue requires responders to have such skills as hiking, skiing, mountain climbing, backcountry navigation, and survival training. First-aid knowledge is vital.

Wilderness search and rescue teams train in tracking. They also learn where a lost person is likely to be found. For example, lost hunters tend to follow water. Berry pickers usually go uphill. Many wilderness SAR personnel work with dogs to aid in searches.

URBAN SAR

Urban search and rescue teams are called in when there are disasters in cities. They help victims trapped in collapsed buildings. Urban SAR teams go to work after there has been an earthquake, tornado, hurricane, or flood. They also help out after terrorist activities and hazardous material accidents.

Urban SAR teams
search for victims in
each house or building in
an area. Rescuers mark
places they've searched
with a red "X."

*Many urban SAR
teams have dogs
to help find people
in collapsed
buildings.*

During an emergency, trained urban SARs
team up with police and fire department first
responders. Additional help often comes from
FEMA (Federal Emergency Management
Agency), the National Guard, and other military

CANINE SAR

A canine search and rescue team includes one handler and one dog. Dogs use their advanced sense of smell to find survivors in remote locations or who are buried in rubble or avalanches. Canines can search at night since they are using their noses, not their eyes. The sooner a search begins, the more likely a person can be found. A friendly furry face is a welcome sight to many victims.

XTREME FACT – The most common search and rescue dog breeds are Labrador retrievers, German shepherds, Belgian Malinois, border collies, and golden retrievers.

Canine SAR handlers train with their dogs for up to two years to become field-ready. Dogs learn that human odor equals a treat.

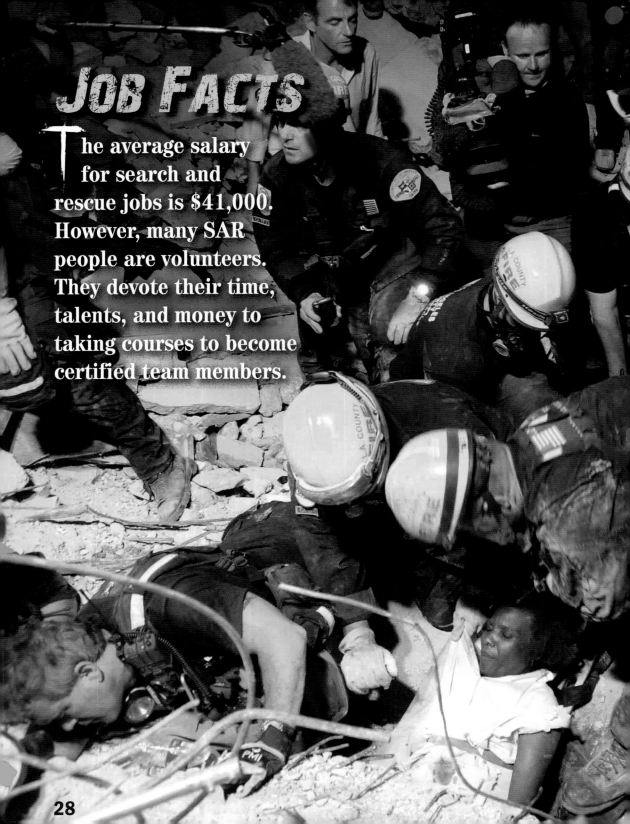

JOB FACTS

The average salary for search and rescue jobs is $41,000. However, many SAR people are volunteers. They devote their time, talents, and money to taking courses to become certified team members.

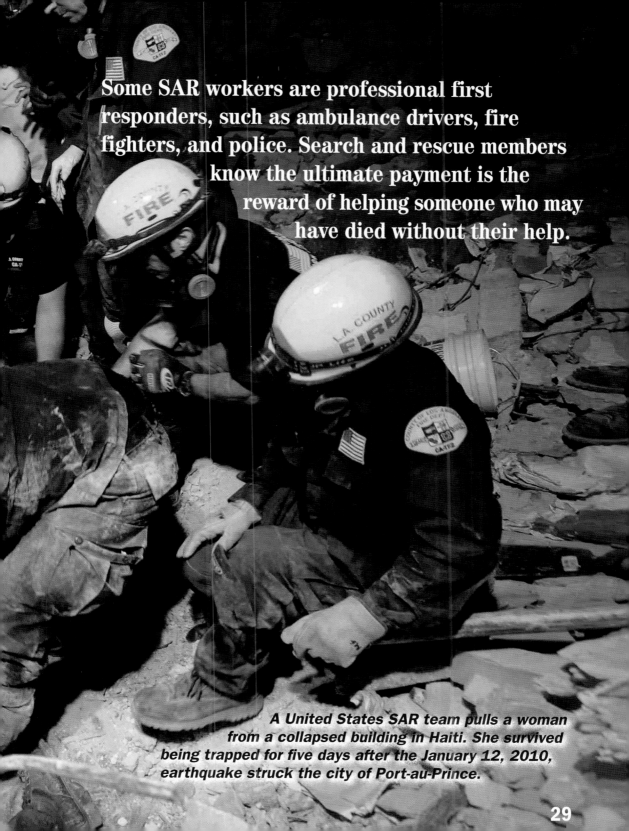

Some SAR workers are professional first responders, such as ambulance drivers, fire fighters, and police. Search and rescue members know the ultimate payment is the reward of helping someone who may have died without their help.

A United States SAR team pulls a woman from a collapsed building in Haiti. She survived being trapped for five days after the January 12, 2010, earthquake struck the city of Port-au-Prince.

GLOSSARY

ALTITUDE
How high a person or object is from the ground or sea level.

DRY SUIT
A waterproof, rubber suit worn over warm clothing and designed to keep a person from getting wet.

FIRST RESPONDERS
People such as police, firefighters, ambulance drivers, emergency medical technicians (EMTs), and paramedics, who are the first on the scene of an emergency situation.

GEOLOGY
The features, especially in rocks, that make up an area on the Earth. Caves may be made up of limestone, dolomite, gypsum, salt, marble, and other materials. The geology of the cave determines how a search and rescue operation proceeds.

HAZARDOUS MATERIAL
Any material that could cause illness or death to people, animals, or plants.

HYPOTHERMIA

When a person's body temperature drops low enough that their brain and muscles cannot function properly. This occurs in wet and/or cold conditions. A person can die from hypothermia.

PARARESCUEMEN

A division of the U.S. Air Force that performs search and rescue of civilians and military personnel. The name "para" comes from the fact that originally the team would parachute into an area to conduct rescues.

SPELUNKER

A person who explores caves.

SWIFTWATER

Also known as whitewater. Fast-moving water that runs at a speed of at least 1.24 miles per hour (2 kph).

TRAUMA MEDICINE

Medical treatment for severe injuries to the body.

UNCONSCIOUS

A person who is not awake or aware of what is going on around them.

INDEX